NATURE, ROCKS, & MINERALS

A Biblical Perspective

"Speak to the earth and it will teach you." Job 12:8

GOD THE FATHER -Designs (Jeremiah 10:12)
THE SON OF GOD - JESUS -Creates (Ephesians 3:9)
THE HOLY SPIRIT - Quickens (Colossians 1:27)

[GOD'S SECOND BOOK]

WestBow Press books may be ordered through booksellers or by contacting:

WestBow Press
A Division of Thomas Nelson & Zondervan
1663 Liberty Drive
Bloomington, IN 47403
www.westbowpress.com
1 (866) 928-1240

ISBN: 978-1-4908-3435-1 (sc)
ISBN: 978-1-4908-3434-4 (e)

Library of Congress Control Number: 2014907289

Printed in the United States of America.

WestBow Press rev. date: 02/06/2015

WestBow
PRESS
A DIVISION OF THOMAS NELSON
& ZONDERVAN

CONTENTS

ACKNOWLEDGMENTS

There have been many influences that led me to write this book. I realized that when Jesus was teaching His disciples, etc. many times He would use examples in Nature to make important points. Many were Farmers, He would mention Wheat and Tares. Some were Fisherman, He would talk about fish. " I will make you fishers of men." Matthew 4:18. God said to Job " Where wast thou when I laid the foundations of the earth? Declare, if thou hast understanding." Job 38:4. May we never be tempted to exalt our wisdom above God's. Our way of thinking is different than God's (Bible is Truth). Read (John 17:17; Matthew 4:4 Compare Proverbs 14:12; Isaiah 55:8,9). It was then that I learned the importance of combining God's [First Book] The King James Bible with God's [Second Book] Nature, to get even a deeper understanding of God's Will for my life!   NATURE REVEALS GOD IN A SPECIAL WAY!

I want to Thank God for the gift of the Holy Spirit, which gives the Praying Christian [Abilities] that otherwise would be impossible in their own Wisdom or own Strength. Read (John 14:26). See what Grace can accomplish in our life If we have Faith! Please Read (Titus 2:11,12; 1 John 3:6-9) in the King James Bible. That would remove all our excuses for continued known sinning! Christians submit to a "thus saith The Lord ", then act like we Believe it ! James was very Practical, Logical, we would say- Down to Earth in explaining God's Will: " Wherefore lay apart all filthiness and superfluity of naughtiness, and receive with meekness the engrafted word, which is able to save your souls.But be ye doers of the word, and not hearers only, deceiving your own selves." (James 1:21,22). Read about the Parable of the sower: (Mark 4:1-9) .We [must] allow God to sow The Word in our heart, so we can live it out in our life!

There were abilities lacking in my own life in order to make this book a reality. I thank my dear wife for being Faithful and Patient with me. My knowledge comes from reading The Bible and many years outside studying Nature. I wanted to appreciate more my Creator and learning important lessons, He wanted to teach me. Theresa was my human Dictionary, she's really good at it! She's also my Computer Expert when things Freeze or Go Blank, I don't have to Panic, she knows what to do. Thanks Honey Bun!

DEDICATION

Compared to Eternity with God, life on earth is so short, God's Word calls it a vapor.

"Whereas ye know not what shall be on the morrow, For what is your life? It is even a vapor, that appeareth for a little time, and then vanisheth away." (James 4:14). Please read also (1 Peter 1:24 and Ecclesiastes 1:4).

We prepare ourselves for this temporary world by learning a job so we can make a living. We would have to agree, it makes <u>even more sense</u> to prepare for Eternity with God. That's not Temporary but Permanent!

" Nevertheless we, according to his promise, look for new heavens and a new earth, wherein dwelleth righteousness. Wherefore, beloved, seeing that ye look for such things, <u>be diligent (watchful, on guard)</u> that ye may be found of him in peace, without spot, and blameless." (2 Peter 3:13,14).

In Amos 4:12, God's Word says: " prepare to meet thy God, O, Israel." Paul tells us that" The Israel of God" is Born Again Christians. (Galatians 6:15,16). Read the Bible, enjoy and learn from God's [Second Book] - Nature, and discover what a wonderful Savior and Creator Jesus is. Read (Matthew 1:21; Ephesians 3:9). Our Heavenly Father wants to Adopt us, It is God's Will that all mankind be saved but, it must be ** OUR CHOICE** to make it a reality!

<u>This book is dedicated first, to my Heavenly Father who said</u>: " Come out and be ye separate, saith the Lord, and I will receive you, and be a Father unto you, and ye shall be my sons and daughters." (2 Corinthians 6:17,18). God who is the Creator of all things, certainly can take care of His adopted Created Beings - He wants the Best for all of us! Not just in this Temporary world but for Eternity!

<u>Secondly, this book is dedicated to my family,</u> <u>whom I want so much to be able to spend Eternity with</u>, Friends and you [The Reader]. It's not automatic , we have to make our own Personal Decisions about Jesus. He Loves Us, He's waiting patiently for you and I to Love Him, How ? - Just spend quality time with Him in the Bible, and Nature if possible, By " Beholding we become changed" (2 Corinthians 3:18; Psalm 34:8; Jeremiah 29:11-14). God wants us to have Jesus Character. "For God who commanded the light to shine out of darkness, has shined it in our hearts to give the light of the knowledge of the glory of God in the face of Jesus Christ." (2 Corinthians 4:6). His "face" is His Character! Talking about you and I - " This is the generation of them that seek him, that seek thy (Jesus') face." (Psalm 24:6). It will happen, Jesus is Irresistible! I know, He wants to POLISH US UP , bring the Best out in all of us ,and give us Salvation, if we let Him !

INTRODUCTION

FROM HAVING ROCK HOUND FEVER TO BECOMING A BORN AGAIN CHRISTIAN

This is [Happy Time] , I love talking about Nature, Rocks and Minerals, the Adventure starts now!

I feel like a 1849'r Gold Rush Prospector - I love Hunting for Rocks and Minerals!

Being a Nature Lover - Spring, Summer and Fall I spend a lot of time out doors. I like to Hike (go trailing) or sometimes go Kayaking especially with my grandson Mickey (Adam Jr.) and fellow Nature Lover Jack Dettner, he's COOL! But, in the Winter time - Lord, make me a Bear so I can hibernate, then, wake me up in the Spring! The Holy Spirit whispered in my ear and said, I got a better idea - don't waste this time, <u>write another book, this book,</u> **my life experiences with my Creator!**

Part of my collection of Indian Arrow Heads and Civil War Bullets! (Looked in old Corn Fields after a rain, etc.

It started over forty years ago in Brunswick, Maryland, my grandfather Clarence Elvin Streight started me hunting for Indian Arrow Heads and Civil War Bullets at Harper's Ferry, West Va. What a wonderful Hobby and Earthy Treasures to be Discovered! As I got older I went to Rock and Mineral shows and then started Exploring Mines and Quarries, etc. I especially enjoyed going to Mt Ida, Arkansas to mine for beautiful Quartz Crystals, here's a sample of what I found:

Quartz Crystal mined at Mt. Ida, Arkansas

Herkimer Diamond in Matrix (Mother Rock)

At Crystal Grove Mine - New York, I chiseled Lime Stone discovering Herkimer Diamonds, they only have a hardness of [7] but, they look like Real Diamonds beautifully cut by God - what a wonderful experience! I didn't realize what was happening to me, I came down with Rock Hound Fever. Be careful, it is very contagious, a lot of my friends have it too! It has affected me in a very Positive way, ** <u>my wife? She didn't catch Rock Hound Fever</u> **, her experience can best be explained by a Poem - by an unknown Author, Enjoy !

Rock Hound Fever

"There's a strange kinda fever that's going around, anyone can get it, it's called Rock hound, It really is disastrous for the rock hound's wife for she's got a rival for the rest of her life.

When Rick gets a nice vacation, does he take her out? No, He'll grab a pick and hammer to the mountains he'll go. When she meets him at the door and expects a little kiss, Hubby holds out a rock and says, "Hey, look at this Quartz Crystal, look at this piece of Pyrite." !

There are rocks in the kitchen, on the couch, and floor, the house is [caving in] but he brings in more. Theresa starts to wash the dishes, but what do you think? Rick's washing minerals in the kitchen sink.

There are rubies, emeralds, Herkimer diamonds lying around but she hasn't got a love, Rick's just an old Rock hound. When he turns out the light and gets into bed, Theresa can almost hear those rocks rolling around in his head. - Can a man keep his wife and marry a rock also? Theresa said 'No!' One more rock and I'm gone, don't ya know!" - The End .

My wife Theresa would say - I'm going overboard with all these Rocks, I need to be more balanced, I'm Praying to God " give us a little revival in our bondage ." (Ezra 9:8).

When I became a Christian and developed a love for reading The King James Bible [God's First Book] I experienced the miracle of being Born Again. Problems don't go away, Jesus gives us Solutions to ours problems. When I look at myself- I don't see how I can be saved. When I look at Jesus- I cannot see how I can be lost! God's Word explains it like this: " Being born again, not of corruptible seed, but incorruptible by the word of God, which liveth and abideth forever." (1 Peter 1: 23). David said this about Jesus: " O taste and see that the LORD is good: blessed is the man that trusteth in him." (Psalm 34:8). I took David's advice and started reading the Gospels - Matthew, Mark, Luke and John - I realized for the first time what a wonderful Savior Jesus is. He correctly showed mankind His Father's Loving Character, healed people, taught His disciples God's Will for their lives, gave us an example of what we as Christians should do to prepare for Eternity and died on Calvary's Cross that - If we Believe in Him, our Salvation from sin, not in sin is Assured .Read (2 Timothy 2:19). You Too, can learn about Jesus, He's Great!

In case you were wondering, Yes, Theresa and I are still married. Jesus brings out the Best in all of us, even [us] Hard Headed, Rocks in our Head ** Rock Hounds ** Ha! Ha!

I found out that there is a close relationship between God and Nature, and wonderful lessons to be learned, the Bible says this: " Speak to the earth and it will teach you." Job 12:8. Nature is God's [Second Book]. Before sin existed, God Created this earth through His Son, Jesus Christ. The Apostle Paul says: " And to make all men see what is the fellowship of the mystery, which from the beginning of the world hath been hid in God, who created all things by Jesus Christ." (Ephesians 3:9) KJ Bible. " And God saw everything that he had made, and behold, it was very good. (Genesis 1:31).. " He created it not in vain, He formed it to be inhabited." (Isaiah 45:18). God made this Earth especially for You and I : " Yea, I have loved thee with an everlasting love, therefore with loving kindness I have drawn thee ". (Jeremiah 31:3).

It is my Prayer that through reading the Bible [God's First Book] and studying Nature [God's Second Book] we will all see how much our Heavenly Father loves us and is drawing us close to Him as our Creator and Re-Creator. Paul explains it like this: " Therefore if any man be in Christ, he is a new creature: old things are passed away (the self-centered sinful life); behold, all things have become new." (2 Corinthians 5:17). This change is so evident that God's Word says we become "another man" (1 Samuel 10:6). A Spiritual man " For to be carnally minded is death; but to be spiritually minded is life and peace. For as many as are led by the Spirit of God, they are the sons of God." (Romans 8:6,14). A new Born Again man "Which are born, not of blood , nor will of the flesh, nor will of man, but of God Jesus said this: " Verily, verily, I say unto thee, Except a man be born again, he cannot see the kingdom of God." (John 1:13; 3:3). Jesus said Verily, verily twice, Being Born Again is very important! We are to be no longer Worldly minded but, Spiritually minded. Nolonger feeding the Flesh but feeding the Spirit! Paul said this to the Brethren: " If ye then be risen with Christ, seek those things which are above, where Christ setteth on the right hand of God. Set your affection on things above, not on things on the earth." (Colossions 3:1,2) " But now they desire a better country, that is, an heavenly: wherefore God is not ashamed to be called their God: for he hath prepared for them a city." (Hebrews 11:16).

GETTING TO KNOW OUR CREATOR - PERSONALLY !

I can only share a few thoughts on this subject, please go to the Library, your Computer, Encyclopedia, etc. and learn more, it is a Fascinating Study!

This Earth will [teach us] just how much God loves us, it shows His Goodness and Watch care Protection towards His created beings. He made Planet Earth very special just for You and I. The King James Bible says this : " For thus saith the LORD that created the heavens; God himself that formed the earth and made it; he has established it, he created it not in vain, he formed it to be inhabited ..." (Isaiah 45:18). As I, Rick Streight, have learned these Facts, my Faith has been Magnified, hope yours will be also! Now lets ** DIVE ** into [God's Second Book] Head First, No! I mean <u>Mind First</u>, <u>Heart First</u>!

LOVE YOUR CREATOR! MY CREATOR! OUR CREATOR!

Our Creator of the Heaven and Earth is Awesome, Magnificent, Beautiful ! " He hath made the earth by HIS POWER. He hath established the world by HIS WISDOM, and has stretched out the heavens by HIS DISCRETION. " Jeremiah 10:12

Relating to God, Psalm 8:1 says: " O LORD our Lord, how excellent is thy name in all the earth! who hast set thy glory above the heavens."   I can Trust my Creator and Re- Creator!

Ghost Crabs at night on the beach of Outer Banks , N.C. Need a flash light to find them.

Lysa feeding Sea Gulls at O B X]

**Lysa in Ocean City , Maryland . I like Rocks, but I love my daughter
[much more]. Smile Lysa, you are a great joy in my life!**

My [good looking] grandson Mickey , he's also a Nature Lover - Beautiful
Water Fall at Susquehanna State Park , Maryland

My wife Theresa at Harper's Ferry, West Va. Jesus and Nature brings
out the Best in all of us, Honey, you look Great!]

My wife Theresa, with our daughter Lysa, on Interstate Highway California going toward San Diego . Notice the Beautiful snow capped mountains above the clouds, Awesome! Only God can Create such Beauty!

Beautiful Sunflower fields, Summer of 2013 Jarrettsville, MD. As Beautiful as these flowers are, they have been [degenerated] for 6,000 years. In The New Heaven and New Earth - <u>all things</u> will be so much more Beautiful!

"For since the beginning of the world men have not heard, nor perceived by the ear, neither hath the eye seen, O God, beside thee, what he hath prepared for him that waiteth for him." (Isaiah 64:4) Read also (1 Corinthians 2:9, 10). There are Great Benefits of being a Christian, In this world as well as in Eternity, Thank You Jesus!

This Red Bud Tree is in my back yard, it gets pink blooms on branches before
the purple leaves form later in the Spring., unusual, but very Beautiful

My daughter Lysa and her husband Evangelist Juan Rivera. They are Nature Lovers
like myself.We all must learn precious lessons here on earth to prepare for Eternity
with God. The Bible, Nature and life experiences are great teachers!

SUNSHINE, AIR, WATER, FOOD, OUR ATMOSPHERE ABOVE AND EARTH BELOW - OUR WISE, POWERFUL AND LOVING CREATOR!

1. **The Sun** - it gives us Day light, Warmth and Reflection on the moon at night. God put the Sun just exactly where we need it the most. If it was farther away- we would freeze to death, closer - we would burn up because of the intense heat. We can Trust our Creator God, He knows how to take care of us! Can we survive without His Help? No! We all depend on our Creator, may we all show our appreciation! LOVE HIM, AND WORSHIP HIM! Read (Revelation 14:7).

2. **Our Atmosphere Protects Us and Supplies many of our needs!** - Every day Planet Earth is bombarded with Tons of Meteorites and other particles from Outer Space. God gave our atmosphere a protective shield of friction which burns them up. Our atmosphere also supplies us with life giving water from the ocean to our land masses. The Sun evaporates water into the air, purifies it, then carries the [water vapor] to land as rain or snow depending on temperature. God made this Earth specifically for mankind to live, taking care of all our needs, Because He Loves Us!

3. **The Surface of the Earth** has been designed [on purpose] by God with mountains and valleys. If the surface or crust of the earth was originally flat or became flat, Earth would be under water deeper than a mile, No land life - Humans or animals could not live. Again, Our Heavenly Father made this Earth especially for You and I. He wants us to Trust Him, He wants us to Love Him and Read the Bible, putting on " the mind of Christ " Philippians 2:5 . Putting on His Power (Philippians 4:13).

4. **God Created this World by His Spoken Word** In (Genesis Chapter 1) We read about God's Creation week and His Power to make it a reality! It took six 24 hour days and then God rested on the Sabbath, Read (Exodus 20:11; Revelation 14:7). How Powerful is God's Word? When God speaks, His Word makes it happen. " By the word of the LORD the heavens were made and all the host of them by the breath of his mouth. Let all the earth fear the LORD: let all the inhabitants (includes you and I) of the world stand in awe of him . <u>For he spake, and it was done; he commanded, and it stood fast.</u>" (Psalms 33:6,9). The Word of God has that same power all through the Bible, if we have the Faith that God wants us to have. ** He wants us To Believe Him, and Act on that Belief ** . We are forgiven of our sins (1 John 1:9) **Because He said so**! We are Empowered (Philippians 4:13; 1 Corinthians 10:13; Jude 24; Psalms 119:11) **Because He said so!** When God put His Moral Law (The Ten Commandments) in our hearts (Hebrews 8:10 ; Psalm 40:7,8) He gives us the Power to love Him, love our fellow man and resist any Temptation Satan wants to throw at us. **Because He said so!** " We love Him because he first loved us." (1 John 4:19).

The Bible says this: " Our Father which art in heaven, hallowed be thy name. Thy kingdom come. Thy will be done in earth, as it is in heaven. " (Matthew 6:9,10).

[There are Three Heavens]

1. Our Atmosphere where Birds and Air Planes fly, experience Rain and Sunshine is The First Heaven. Read (Genesis 1:8; Deuteronomy 28:12; Ps. 104:12).

2. Our Universe where the Sun, Moon, Stars and other Planets are is The Second Heaven Read (Psalms 8:3,4).

3. Our Heavenly Father lives Beyond the others, God Dwells in The Third Heaven Read (1 Corinthians 2:9,10). Satan and his Third of the angels were cast out of heaven and sent to the Earth. Read also (Revelations 12:3,4; 2 Corinthians 4:4) " The LORD is in his holy temple, the LORD'S Throne is in heaven: his eyes behold, his eyelids try (Test) the children of men (You and I)." Psalm 11:4 .

God's Character, His Government is based on LOVE. " Beloved, let us love one another: for love is of God; and everyone that loveth is born of God, and knoweth God. He that loveth not knoweth not God; for God is love." (1 John 4:7,8). Read also (1 Corinthians 13th Chapter).

Again, Matthew 6:10 says: " Thy kingdom come. Thy will be done in earth, as it is in heaven." [The Third Heaven]. God is telling You and I, if we want to go to heaven, by God's Grace and Power we need Jesus to help us apply God's Government of LOVE to our lives **Now**, be a Blessing to all we come in contact with **Now**, Witness for Jesus - **Now**, Overcome Sin -**Now!** Read (Revelation 22:11-14) The above Scripture tells us Probation for mankind ends at Death, Jesus Second Coming or when we no longer can discern between Right or Wrong. " Then shall ye (Jesus) return, and discern between the righteous and the wicked, between them that serveth God and him that serveth him not." (Malachi 3:18).

What are the Blessings of being a Faithful and True Christian? By reading God's Word and putting on "the mind of Christ" (Philippians 2:5) We will love God and our fellow man [love the man, witness to the man, hate the sin] Read John 3:17. In the New Testament Jesus gave us Two Great Commandments that sum up all of His Ten Commandment Moral Law. " ...the first of all the commandments is, Hear, O Israel: The Lord our God is one Lord: And thou shalt love the Lord thy God with all thy heart, and with all thy soul, and with all thy mind, and with all thy strength: this is the first commandment. And the second is is like, namely this, Thou shalt love thy neighbor as thy self. There is no other commandment greater than these." (Mark 12: 29-31). " ...love is the fulfilling of the law." (Romans 13:10).

THERE IS ALSO BEAUTY INSIDE THE EARTH [GOD'S CREATION] CRYSTAL GROTTO CAVERNS, BOONESBORO, MARYLAND .

My Precious <u>Jewels </u>Mickey and Julsie.

My precious Crystal may be a beginner, but, learns fast! I'm glad she enjoys Kayaking and the out doors which include Hiking (Trailing), seeing animals like deer, turtles, frogs, squirrels, eagles, etc.

Love it - fresh air, exercise, a peacefulness of being in God's Second Book, Nature.
Actually, a nice break from this sin sick world, Thank you Jesus!

Julsie Girl and Mickey - what kid wouldn't like Kayaking and Swimming in cool Spring fed waters on a Beautiful hot summer day ? I love watching the innocence of children .

My son Adam and his wife Amy at Ocean City, Maryland. year 2014. Nature brings out the Best in all of us. Enjoyment, Peace, an escape from this sinful world, Thank You Jesus!

[God's Second Book]

"But ask now the beasts, and they shall teach thee; and the fowls (birds) of the air, and they shall teach thee: Or speak to the earth, and it shall teach thee; and the fishes of the sea shall declare unto thee." (Job 12:7, 8). The Apostle Paul says this: " For the invisible things of him from the creation of the world are clearly seen (Nature), being understood by the things that are made, even his eternal power and Godhead; so that they (worldly people) are without excuse." (Romans 1:20) NATURE REVEALS GOD. Those that have never seen a Missionary or Preacher can see God's Creation , Everyone is- Without Excuse!

About three miles from my house is Susquehanna State Park. When the weather is good, I love going Hiking there and don't miss the opportunity to Pray, asking God to show me Object Lessons in Nature to make me a Stronger, more Mature Christian, [Reader] He can do the same for you. I have realized that the only way we can be Victorious Christians and be Faithful Witnesses for Jesus is -DO NOT TRUST SELF (Proverbs 14:12)! Our only hope is constant Prayer and Bible Study so we can develop more " the mind of Christ ." (Philippians 2:5) and have " the faith of Jesus " (Revelation 14:12). Nature is also another source of Spiritual Wisdom and Strength, there are many lessons, these are some of the ones God showed me. God will also show you ones [tailor made] for your particular needs and encouragement. Always Pray and ask God for Wisdom to see His Object Lessons!

1. **Be like an Oak Tree** - it was one of those days when Trials and Disappointments came into my life - dear reader, have you ever had days like that? As a Christian, I knew I needed added Prayer and Scripture meditation so I could maintain that " peace that surpasses all understanding." (Philippians 4:7). Jesus is always there in our time of need. The Lord and I needed special time together. I went to The Park - [Prayers are longer] and to my surprise, God gave me an Object Lesson, Thank you Jesus! While taking a Hike in the woods, I saw a large Maple Tree fallen down and noticed how shallow it's roots were, heavy rains and winds knocked it down. Very few Oak Trees fall down because they have Strong and Deep roots like a carrot. **Object Lesson:** Heavy rains and Winds represent Temptations, Disappointments, or Trials in our life. As a Christian we are to be Rooted in Jesus! If our roots are shallow - lack of Prayers and Bible Study - [Jesus can't help us] and we fall into sin or over react, wishing we didn't! Safe Ground- Stay Close to Jesus. The Oak Tree with Strong Deep Roots - the Wind and Rain does not effect it! Total Victory is maintained along with " that peace that surpasses all understanding." (Philippians 4:7). Lord Thank you for that Nature Object Lesson.

2. **A Large Rock Formation in the River** - I enjoy being in Nature, it is with exciting sweet anticipation that I always ask God for another Object Lesson to Strengthen my relationship even more with Jesus! I have walked this trail many times before and never noticed this particular Object Lesson, today was Special! Looking out in the Susquehanna River I saw a large Rock Formation. At the top of it was Pure White, the gates were closed at the Conowingo Dam, the River was low and I noticed the lower sides and base of the Rock was brown, dark in color. **Object Lesson:** When they open the gates at the Conowingo Dam, Dirty, Polluted water rises and makes the large [white] Quartzite Rock look brown. Paul says this in God's Word: " But put ye on the Lord Jesus Christ, and make not provision for the flesh, to fulfill the lusts thereof." Romans 13:14 . To expand on this thought Paul also says: " Be not deceived, God is not mocked: for whatsoever a man soweth, that shall he also reap. For he that soweth to the flesh shall of the flesh reap corruption; but he that soweth to the Spirit shall of the Spirit reap life everlasting." Galatians 6:7,8. When we allow our minds to be Polluted and made dirty by beholding the perversions, wickedness and violence on the TV, at the Movie Theaters, and reading worldly magazines, God's Word is telling us we are on Dangerous ground. Jesus wants us to be good stewards of our mind, eyes and ears. That we can be Victorious Christians over sin and Faithful Witnesses to God's Glory! Like the original Large white Quartz Rock, Jesus wants us to stay clean, pure, " white as snow " Isaiah 1:18. He wants us to Feed the Spirit and Starve the Flesh! " For to be carnally (worldly) minded is death; but to be Spiritually minded is life and peace." Romans 8:6 .Trust God, He is Preparing us to spend Eternity with Him in Heaven. Read (Psalms 25:21 ; Revelation 19:7).

3. **Daddy Goose - Protector of His Family** - This time I was walking on a Trail close to Susquehanna River and very unexpectedly I was confronted by a large Male Goose, he practically got up in my face and STOOD HIS GROUND! You see, behind him, mother goose was walking her baby geese across the Trail going down to the river. The male Goose was protecting his family even unto death until they were safely beyond danger -- Me! Then he backed away and went with his wife and children. I was thrilled by the experience. **Object Lesson:** " There hath no temptation taken you but such as is common to man: but God is Faithful, who will not suffer you to be tempted above that ye are able; but will with the temptation also make a way to escape, that ye may be able to bear it." 1 Corinthians 10:13. " Yea are of God, little children, and have overcome them (temptations): because greater is he (Jesus) that is in you, than he (Satan) that is in the world." 1 John 4:4 If we are Faithful in our Devotional life- Praying and Studying God's Word keeping our Spiritual Armour on (Ephesians 6:10-18), God is our Strength, like the male Goose, He will fight and protect us also from Satan's Attacks. Faith is our Victory (1 John 5:4)- Do we Believe God [can do] what He said He can do ?

4. **April Showers!** On April 29, 2014. I was exercising at the Arena Health Club in Churchville, Maryland. And suddenly I heard a lot of heavy rain coming down, God wanted to teach [you and I] something! **Object Lesson:** In Spring, the weather gets warmer. We as Christians need to be warm at heart, willing to have a hunger for the Truths of God's Word, knowing that Jesus is " The water of life." Revelation 22:17. The Beloved John says this about Jesus: " But whosoever drinketh of the water

that I shall give him shall never thirst; but the water that I shall give him shall be in him a well of water springing up into everlasting life." John 4:14. As I observed the April Showers, Nature and see the Trees and Plants Grow, Bloom and Mature, so it is with [us] Believers. When we allow Jesus "the water of life" help us grow and mature Spiritually, then we also Bloom into Strong Christians and Faithful Witnesses for Jesus. When there is a drought [long periods of no rain] things die, so would we Spiritually if we stopped reading the Bible- " the water of life" The Apostle Paul says: " Keep the Armour of God on " (Ephesians 6:10-18), so we can live and not die Spiritually! Lord, to whom shall we go? thou hast the words of eternal life." (John 6:68).

5. **Our Creator takes care of You and I.** " Behold the fowls of the air: for they sow not, neither do they reap, nor gather into barns; yet your heavenly Father feedeth them. <u>Are ye not much better than they?</u> " (Matthew 6:26). Please Read the other Scriptures : (Matthew 6:25-34). Jesus paid the penalty of sin for us, not for the Lilies, Animals or Birds. We can be sure of His Love for us, regardless of the circumstances. He supplies Rain, Sunshine and Food for [the worldly] as well as [His Faithful Believers]. "Every good gift and every perfect gift is from above, and cometh down from the Father of lights, with whom is no variableness, neither shadow of turning." (James 1:17). God loves us so much, He is longing for us to appreciate all the wonderful things He gives us. Our health, the food we eat, our jobs, our family, our homes, and every blessing [all] come from God.The sun which gives us warmth and light; trees; flowers; rain; our ability to produce offspring (our children also a gift from God) ; our ability to reason, make choices, and solve problems, our eyesight; our hearing; even our Trials are a gift from God, Read (Romans 8:28; 1 Peter 1:7; Revelation 3:19). God provides all these and more for our benefit. Most of all, God offered us Salvation (Grace) so we may be Re-United back into a right relationship with Him. That is also a wonderful gift from God. He Abundantly gives us His Love in so many ways! God is waiting patiently for <u>Our Love</u>, <u>Our Heart</u>, He wants us to spend Eternity with Him. Jesus made that possible ! He's our example in all things : "For even hereunto were ye called: because Christ also suffered for us, <u>leaving us an example,</u> <u>that ye should follow his steps</u>: Who did no sin, neither was guile (deceit) found in his mouth: Who when he was reviled (called bad names) , reviled not again; when he suffered, he threatened not; but committed himself to him that judgeth righteously: Who his own self bare our sins in his own body on the tree (Calvary), that we, <u>being dead to sins</u> (a dead man can't sin), should live unto righteousness: by whose stripes ye are healed. For ye were as sheep going astray; but are now returned unto the Shepherd and Bishop of your souls." (1 Peter 2:21-25). Relating to "being dead to sins" Read also (Romans 6:1-4,6,18).

6. **The Ocean is Powerful and Deep.** Our oceans cover almost three fourths of the earth's surface, it is huge! But, it cannot sink a ship until the water gets into the ship! **Object Lesson**: The negativity of this world cannot cause someone to sin until we allow the world to get inside of us! Stay close to Jesus - A promise in God's Word : " I pray not that thou shouldest take them out of the world, but that thou shouldest <u>keep (protect) them from the evil</u>. (John 17:15).

These are our Siamese Cats, Sealy and Sunny - they have been loved ever sense birth. -very affectionate , We give love- we receive love!

My daughter Lysa's dog, Leona, had nine pups. God puts it in animals also to Protect, Love and take care of their babies.

all our cats have taken an interest in Rocky, the male squirrel!

My precious grand daughter Alison holding a beautiful Toucan Bird near San Cristobal de Las Casas, Mexico. May 31, 2013.

Note: Rocks and Minerals in all their Beauty, formed and shaped by God are just waiting to be Discovered and Enjoyed by man. Thousands of years in hiding, <u>it is an intimacy with God</u> to search and find His Treasures, what a mystery, what a challenge, what a wonderful hobby!

I have experienced the Joy and Excitement of going to Mines and Quarries and finding some of these precious minerals! Imagine chiseling Lime Stone and opening a cavity exposing a Herkimer Diamond that has been hidden in a tome for Thousands of years and God allowed me or you [the Reader] to be the first person to discover it in all it's Beauty!   Got Rock Hound Fever Yet?

Jefferson Rock Cave
Harpers Ferry, W.Va.

A Few Rock Jokes - For Fun! 1. What is a Christian Geologist's favorite music? <u>G</u><u>ospel Rock</u>! 2. What did one rock say to another rock? <u>Don't take me for granite</u>! 3. Are all Geode Rocks so ugly? <u>No, I'm beautiful on the inside where it counts!</u>

Arundel Quarry- Havre de Grace, MD. Not hard to find veins or cubes of Pyrite (Fools Gold). When the sun is shining it sparkles, I love Treasure Hunting in Nature!

Large Pyrite (Fool's Gold). What a disappointment when they found out it wasn't really Gold!] God's Word warns us about Deceptions!

Herkimer Diamonds, Copper ore, Beryl, Pyrite (Fool's Gold) and Amethyst Crystals.

Golden Beryl

At Holtwood Dam, Pa. While Kayaking, discovered this huge Rock Formation with a vein of Quartzite, very interesting!

"In God is my Salvation...the Rock of my Strength."
(Psalm 62:7)

NATURE'S BEAUTY

ROCKS • MINERALS • FLOWERS • TREES • ANIMALS

Nature gives us more opportunities to be intimate with our Creator and be more willing to be Recreated in Christ Jesus. "Therefore if any man be in Christ, he is a new creature, old things are passed away; behold, all things are become new." (2 Corinthians 5:17).

Observe these beautiful Geodes - plain rocks on the outside, beautiful on the inside. By beholding Jesus in God's Word- Read (John 1:1-3,14) Like the Geodes, we too can become Beautiful on the inside. Read (2 Corinthians 3:17,18; Isaiah 13:12). "By Beholding we become changed." Precious in God's sight!

Copper ore.

Henry my pet snake also protects this Beautiful Mica Rock I mined at Coatsville, Pa.

Opal mineral in Mother Matrix Rock

"And I heard a great voice out of heaven saying, Behold, the Tabernacle of God is with men, and he will dwell with them, and they shall be his people, and God himself shall be with them, and be their God."(Revelation 21:3).

" And the building of the wall of it was as jasper: and the city was pure gold, like unto clear glass. And the foundations of the wall of the city were garnished with all manner of precious stones. The first foundation was jasper, the second sapphire; the third, a chalcedony; the fourth, an emerald; The fifth, sardonyx; the sixth, sardius; the seventh, chrysolite; the eighth, beryl; the ninth, topaz; the tenth, a chrysoprasus; the eleventh, a jacinth; the twelfth, an amethyst. And the twelve gates were twelve pearls; every several gate was of one pearl; and the street of the city was pure gold, as it were transparent glass." (Revelation 21:18-21).

Please note: not a Bible inspired statement but, if you [the Reader] don't like Rocks and Minerals, looks like you will be surrounded with such Beauty spending Eternity with God. Now is the time to change your mind. Christians should like what God likes ! ** I'm in Good Company **.

Please note again: We all love Jesus - Jesus was and is **The Pearl of Great Price!**

" Again, the kingdom of heaven is like unto a merchant man, seeking goodly pearls: who, when he had found one pearl of great price (Jesus), went and sold all he had, and bought it. " (Matthew 13: 45,46). What is the Price we are willing to pay? Read (Matthew 16:24; 1 Peter 1:22; Philippians 4:9).

We are also a **Pearl of Great price!** Jesus went to Calvary to purchase You and I. Read (1 Peter 1:18,19; 1 Peter 4:1; Hebrews 2:9) He paid for us, May we give ourselves to Him! He's our Redeemer, Creator, Lord and Savior! If not, we will have to pay the penalty of our own sins. Read (Isaiah 59:1,2; Romans 6:23). Not a good idea; Our problem would be, we don't have the Power to Resurrect our self, Jesus is our only Solution - We should run to Him, Jesus brings out the Best in all of us! Can anyone say A-men! How about a Double A-men! I can Trust God for my Eternity! Not Satan, He's Bad, He's behind all the Suffering and Pain that exists in this world! Read the book of - Job - for Explanation! Satan is a Big Time Rascal, A Dangerous One! " the god of this world . " (2 Corinthians 4:4). Good Advice, Read (James 4: 7,8; Matthew 6:24) We cannot serve God and Satan. We Choose - GOD OR SATAN!

INTERESTING ROCK FACTS !

1. How can we take Rock and reshape it into any size we want to?

A. Cement - (Granite, high Calcium content Limestone & Silica Gravel .

2. What is an invisible solid you can see everyday?

A. Glass. Especially when you clean it with Windex glass cleaner .

3. What kind of Rocks come from Outer Space?

A. Meteorites - (Iron and Stone) For same size - Higher Density than earthly rocks, weighs more!

4. What are the Hardest and Softest known Minerals?

A. Diamond - Hardness of 10 : (Greek for Invincible).
B. Graphite - Softest- Hardness of 2. --Lead pencils use graphite!
C. Both come from the same material - Carbon, which is originally from Plant life. Right set of circumstances of Heat and Pressure creates the Diamond .

5. Pyrite - (Fools Gold) is really Iron and Sulfur

A. Under Pressure - Pyrite will crush - can smell the sulfur.
B. Under Pressure - Real Gold is soft - will flatten . Presently worth about $1,400.00 an ounce.

6. Formation of Petrified Wood :

A. Petrified means to - turn into stone. When trees turn into stone we call it Petrified Wood. A hot Silica -rich solution saturates the wood and gradually a change takes place, the Silica replaces the wood, hardens and preserves the structure of the wood's grain, growing rings, and also insect burrows! Rotting of the wood no longer takes place because it is no longer wood.

7. What Rock can Float in water?

A. Pumice - Volcanic Ash - Very light density! (lighter than water)

8. What is God's most Precious and Valuable Jewel in all the world?

A. YOU and I "And they shall be mine, saith the Lord of hosts, in that day when I make up my Jewels"

(Malachi 3:17). " I will make a man more precious than fine gold; even a man than the golden wedge of Ophir." (Isaiah 13:12) We are so Valuable to God, He wants <u>us</u> to spend Eternity with Him.

" Let your light so shine before men, that they may see your good works, and glorify your Father which is in heaven." (Matthew 5:16) . King Solomon says it like this: " As in water face answereth to face, so the heart of man to man." (Proverbs 27:19).

<u>In Man's Eyes</u> - Gold, Silver, Precious Rocks and Minerals are Beautiful and worth a lot of money, etc. They even exalt our Creator, but, the Wisdom we get through Prayer, The Holy Spirit (John 16:13 ;John 14:26) And Daily Bible Study, In God's Eyes is far more Precious than Rocks and Minerals. He wants to Polish us up like Geodes, then, we will be Beautiful and Precious [on the inside], our Character will be like Jesus and God will be Glorified.

<u>Spiritual Growth is more important than silver or gold</u>: "Receive my instruction, and not silver; and knowledge rather than choice gold. For wisdom is better than rubies; and all the things that may be desired are not to be compared with. For whosoever findeth me findeth life, and shall obtain favour of the Lord ." (Proverbs 8: 10,11,35).Read also v.36.

" Who can find a virtuous (pure, righteous) woman? Her price is far above rubies. The heart of her husband doeth safely trust her, so that he shall have no spoil. " (Proverbs 31: 10,11). If we obey God's Word, we [can] develop a Christ -like Character. **Here are our instructions, the How Too! God's Way**! " Now the Lord is that spirit: and where the Spirit of the Lord is, there is liberty. But we all, with open face beholding as in a glass the Glory of the Lord, are changed into the same image (Jesus Character) from glory to glory, even as by the Spirit of the Lord." (2 Corinthians 3:17,18). Philippians 2: 5,15 says this " Let this mind be in you, which was also in Christ Jesus." Verse 15. " That ye may be blameless and harmless, the sons of God, without rebuke, in the midst of a crooked and perverse nation, <u>among whom ye shine as lights in the world</u>." Our Teaching Manual - The King James Bible!

9. **What is the [most] Precious Rock in all the world ? God Himself also Jesus !**

(Psalm 62:6,7) " He, (God), only is my <u>Rock</u> (stability, strength, etc.) and my salvation; He is my defense: I shall not be moved." Verse 7: In God is my salvation and my glory: <u>the Rock of my strength,</u> and my refuge, is in God. " (1 Corinthians 10:4) " And did all drink the same spiritual drink: for they drank of that spiritual Rock that followed them: and that Rock was Christ. " May we Trust in Jesus to be our Lord and Savior " from sin" Matthew 1:21 . [not in sin]. Jesus said this : " With men it is impossible, but not with God: for with God all things are possible ." (Mark 10:27). " For who is God, save the LORD? and who is a rock, save our God? God is my strength and power: and He maketh my way perfect." (2 Samuel 22:32,33). Jesus was " tempted like as we are, yet without sin." (Hebrews 4:15). God was His Rock - He never let go of His Father's Power. We too can be Victorious over [temptations] to God's Glory, if we also stay close to Our Rock- Our Lord- Our Savior- Jesus Christ! "Offer unto God thanksgiving; and pay thy vows unto the most High: And call upon me in the day of trouble: I will deliver thee, and thou shalt glorify me." (Psalm 50:14,15). Anyone can say- Honk your horn if you love Jesus, that's not in the Bible. According to the Scripture we just read, when we resist temptation "the day of trouble" we glorify God. Biblically- when we resist Temptation, we stop [known sinning], James explains it like this: "Whosoever committeth sin transgresseth (breaks) also the law; for sin is the transgression of the law." (1 John 3:4). The more I thought about this Scripture the more I realized that, if sin is breaking the law then, resisting temptation in Christ's strength (Philippians 4:13) is not breaking the law, it would be Keeping God's Commandments because we love our Creator! Jesus said: "If ye love me, keep my commandments. He that hath my commandments, and keepeth them, he it is that loveth me: and he that loveth me shall be loved by my Father, and I will love him, and will manifest (reveal) myself to him." (John 14:15, 21). "My son, forget not my law; but let thine heart keep my commandments: for length of days, and long life, and peace, shall they add to thee. Let not mercy and truth forsake thee: bind them about thy neck; write them upon the table of thine heart. So shalt thou find favour and good understanding in the sight of God and man." (Proverbs 3:1-4). This is Love, not being Legalistic! Would God want Christians who represent Him to Steal, Commit Adultery, use The Lord's Name In Vain, etc.? No! Everyone of God's Commandments is [Loving God] and [Loving our fellow man]. God certainly wants us to Love and Worship Him as our Creator. Please take the time and Read (Genesis 1:1-31; 2:1-3) (Exodus 20:8-11).

Speaking from [My heart to Your heart] I the Author- Rick Streight have shared my Experiences, and Discoveries in God's Word and Nature in hopes that you The Reader would be better Informed and will have a Greater Appreciation of just how Wonderful your Creator is. God's [Second Book] Nature, is Refreshing, Exciting and will teach you- God is all Powerful " Ah Lord GOD! behold, thou hast made the heaven and the earth by thy Great Power and stretched out arm, and there is nothing to hard for thee." (Jeremiah 32: 17). God is all Loving and Cares for You and I: " For I know the plans I have for you, declares the LORD, " plans to prosper you and not to harm you, plans to give you hope and a future. Then ye will call upon me and come and pray with me, and I will listen to you. You will seek me and find me when ye seek me with all your heart. I will be found by you, "declares the LORD and will bring you back from captivity (bondage)." (Jeremiah 29:11-15). " Yea, I (God) have loved thee with an everlasting love, therefore with loving kindness I have drawn thee." (Jeremiah 31:3) " You are precious in my eyes, and honored , and I love you." (Isaiah 43:4). The things that are important to all of us is **[Shared Love]** From Spouses, Children and Respected Friends. Our ability to Love is a gift from God!

God could have made us Robots, we would do everything we were programmed to do, Mechanical, Legal - Obedience [no love involved], **Where would be God's Happiness?** -He wants to be Loved also by His created beings, You and I . His Character is Love- " For God so loved the world, that he gave his only begotten Son, that whosoever believeth in him, should not perish but have everlasting life. For God did not send his Son into the world to condemn the world; but that the world through him (Jesus) might be saved." (John 3:16,17) Read also (1 John 4:7,8). And God said, let us make man in our own image, after our likeness ... ." (Genesis 1:26) Not Robots! Because of HIS LOVE, God gave us FREEDOM OF CHOICE - we could choose to Obey or Dis-Obey our Creator. God gave us Plenty of reason to make the right choice, to LOVE HIM AND OBEY HIM " because he first loved us ." (1 John 4:19). " O taste and see that the Lord is good: blessed is the man that trusteth in him. " (Psalm 34:8), I have experienced this truth: God brings out the Best in all of us, under [all circumstances] and gives us that " peace that surpasses all understanding " (Philippians 4:7). Because of Trials and Disappointments, the world falls apart, but, God gives His Believers -- Peace, Direction in our life, and most importantly, the motivation to want to Worship Our Creator: " Fear God, and give glory to him; for the hour of his judgement is coming: and worship him that made heaven, and earth, and the sea, and the fountains of waters."(Revelation 14:7). To Worship God is to put Him [first] in our life . An Important Principle " He must increase, but I must decrease ." (John 3:30). Read also (2 Corinthians 5:15). May we all read God's Word - The Bible so we can learn more about God's Will for our life and experience the joy of having Jesus as our Personal Lord and Savior from sin! You want to know more about Love? Be better at it? God's The Expert! , He can teach us A LOT about LOVE- He's the AUTHOR OF LOVE! We love our Parents, we love our Brothers and Sisters, special Friends, We should Love Our Creator *** M O R E *** !

1. **Igneous - formed from Magma (molten rock) - Volcanic Lava - Ash (Pumice).**

   A. Granite - Formed deep in the Earth's crust from Magma coming closer to Earth's surface and cooled, hardened!

   B. Igneous rocks can cool slowly deep in the Earth which can develope into Large Crystals, or when forced because of circumstances of pressure, etc. to cooler locations, the Magma closer to the surface of the Earth cools faster forming smaller Crystals, glass formations, etc. Two Groups can combine - (Igneous & Medamorphic Rocks).

2. **Metamorphic - (Greek for Transformation)**

   A. Sandstone can be changed into Crystals - glass, etc.

   B. Coal can be changed into Diamonds (Special circumstances of Heat and Pressure)

   C. Wood can be changed to Petrified Wood

   D. Wood and Plant Life covered over many years of Decay or Pressure can also be changed into Oil, Gas, Coal, etc. Two Groups can combine - (Metamorphic & Sedimentary Rocks).

3. **Sedimentary** --Hardened Mud, Clay, Sandstone, Slate, Coal ,etc.

   A. Fossils - evidence and preservation of former life, plant or animal. Found entombed or trapped in these Rock Formations.

   B. Chalk is found from deposits of Calcite (shelled microscopic organisms that settle to the bottom of the ocean).

   C. Limestone is a very common Rock, made mostly of calcite. Origionally formed in the sea from sediment remains of marine organisms solidified! (Algae, Corals, Shells,etc.). Even though Dry Land, at one time -many or thousands of years ago, Ocean was present! Part of the Universal Flood at Noah's time?

   D. Facts! Sharks Teeth found at Morocco, Africa eighty miles from the closest Ocean.

   E. Corral Fossils in Payson, Arizona. No evidence of Water or Ocean around anywhere?

   F. Where is the Ocean? In the Country of Chile - In a very dry desert [Atacama Region]. fossil marine mammals - Whales, Sharks, Seals, etc. were discovered and dug up. No water anywhere? God is strengthening our Faith in God's Word and He is using Nature to accomplish it. Read (Genesis Chapters 6,7,8). Speak to the Earth and it shall teach thee." Job 12:8. The Bible is Truth, God's [Second Book] Nature proves it!

1. Have you come down with Rock Hound Fever Yet? I'm doing my Best to make it happen! Nice Hobby! and you will get a Better Understanding of your Creator , Hope So !

2. Exercise both body [and] more importantly the mind Spiritually. Paul says this: " For bodily exercise profiteth little: but <u>godliness is profitable unto all things</u>, having promise of the life that now is, and of that which is to come." (1 Timothy 4:8). What is God's Will for our life? The Apostle Paul also says this: "Be not conformed to this world: but be ye transformed by the renewing of your mind, that ye may prove what is that good, and acceptable, and perfect, will of God." (Romans 12:2).

When we do Physical Exercise, we make our body Stronger [Physically]!

My precious daughter Lysa and I having fun exercising at The Arena Club in Churchville, MD. July 2013.

When we do Spiritual Exercise- reading God's Word, we make our mind Strong [Spiritually]!

The Law of Beholding - " Be not deceived; God is not mocked: for whatsoever a man soweth, that shall he also reap. For he that soweth to his flesh shall of the flesh reap corruption; but he that soweth to the Spirit shall of the Spirit reap life everlasting." (Galatians 6:7,8).We can't go down the "Wide and Narrow road" at the same time. (Matthew 7:13,14,18). When we go to Calvary- Christians wouldn't want too, sin becomes repulsive to us, because we love Jesus!

There is a common thread that relates to all mankind. Because of Adam and Eve's Disobedience in the garden of Eden (Genesis Chapter 3) We inherited a fallen Human Nature that makes wrong choices and we sin against God, we become [Sinners in need of a Savior] ! Calvary was necessary to give us " a broken and contrite heart " (Psalms 51:17) so that we would hate sin the way Jesus hates sin and be separated from it. Read (Genesis 3:15) " Enmity " Sin becomes repulsive to us! JESUS BECOMES OUR LOVING SAVIOR, How? We accept Him! What is our Motivation? Our Works? No - **It's The Cross**! Paul the Apostle says this: "For the preaching of the cross is to them that perish foolishness; but unto us which are saved it is the power of God. "(1 Corinthians 1:18). It wasn't just the Jews or the Roman soldiers two thousand years ago who crucified Christ; it was You and I .OUR SINS CRUCIFIED CHRIST " But he ([Jesus] was wounded **for our transgressions**, He was bruised **for our iniquities** (sins): the chastisement of our peace was upon him; and with his stripes we are healed." (Isaiah 53:5). Read also (1 Peter 2:24,25). As we hopefully accept this gift of LOVE, we cry out FORGIVE ME LORD! " Create in me a clean heart, O God; and renew a right spirit within me." (Psalm 51:10). He then Re-Creates us (2 Corinthians 5:17) - He Re-generates us " ...seeing that we have put off **the old man** with his deeds; and have put on **the new man**, which is renewed in knowledge after the image (character) of him (Jesus) that created him". (Colossians 3:9,10). He then motivates us to read God's Word and fall in love with Him. We want His Character to be our Character, we want His Power to be our Power, By Faith in His promises we experience being set free from sin and it's bondage: read (Romans Chapter 8) and enjoy the Liberty we receive in Christ Jesus. read (Philippians 4:13; 1 Corinthians 10:13; Jude 24) "The Truth shall set us free, and we shall be free in deed." (John 8:32,36).

There is hope for the Alcoholic who can't overcome drinking [in his own strength]. There is hope for people that need Victory over Smoking, Over eating, Bad Tempers, Thoughts that are not pleasing to God, read (Philippians 4:8; Psalms 19:14). There is hope for Broken and Unhappy marriages, if we put Jesus first, forgiveness and love can restore marriages that God would be Glorified. Whatever the Addiction is, Jesus can take it away. Read a Prophecy in the Old Testament about Jesus (Isaiah 61:1-3) In the New Testament we read: "But Jesus Beheld them, and said unto them, with men this is impossible, but with God all things are possible." (Matthew 19:26). That's the Good News , that's The Gospel! That's the Great Commission that all Christians are to Witness to the World. Read (Matthew 28:19,20) True Christians will Encourage The World and the Brethren to be Faithful to God and Jesus. The Bible says this: "as iron sharpens iron, so a man sharpeneth the countenance (wits) of a friend." (Proverbs 27:17). We all Witness, either for Jesus or Against Jesus. David says this: "a true witness delivereth souls but a deceitful witness speaketh lies."

(Proverbs 14:25). By God's Grace, Love and Power may we all be TRUE WITNESSES - CHRIST-LIKE WITNESSES! We all know - We get Knowledge and Experience to be an Electrician, We get Knowledge and Experience to be a Nurse, We get Knowledge and Experience to be an Engineer. The Law of Beholding makes it a Reality. Same with becoming a True Christian. From reading The Bible Prayerfully, we get Knowledge, God gives us Experiences and [allows] Trials to come into our life, to Mature us Spiritually! "Sanctify them through thy truth: thy word is truth." (John 17:17) "My son, despise not the chastening of the LORD; neither be weary of his correction: For whom the LORD loveth he correcteth; even as a father the son in whom he delighteth." (Proverbs 3:11,12). "As many as I love, I rebuke and chasten: be zealous therefore, and repent." (Revelation 3:19). "To him that overcometh will I grant to set with me in my throne, even as I (Jesus) also overcame, and am set down with my Father in his throne." (Revelation 3:21). For those that already know, Benefits are Now! Escaping this Sin Sick World and Spending Eternity with God makes all the efforts WORTH IT! can any one say A-Men!" I can "A-Men! Every One has to be given their opportunity! Are we going to say YES or NO to our wonderful Creator?

The Apostle Paul says this: "And that he (Jesus) died for all, that they which live **should not henceforth live unto themselves**, but unto him which died for them, and rose again." (2 Corinthians 5:15). It would be dangerous to hold back from making a [firm] decision about Jesus. Again Paul says: " ...behold now is the accepted time; behold, now is the day of salvation." (2 Corinthians 6:2). Paul is speaking from his heart, he loves the people : " How shall we escape, if we neglect so great salvation; which at the first began to be spoken by the Lord, and was confirmed unto us by them that heard him;" (Hebrews 2:3). Do we really want to say No to the precious gift of Grace Jesus paid at Calvary so our sins could be forgiven? Hope Not! Jesus encourages us, with a sobering and serious reality: " BEHOLD, the LORD'S hand is not shortened, that it cannot save; neither his ear heavy, that it cannot hear: But your iniquities (wickedness, sins) have separated between you and your God, and your sins have hid his face from you, that he will not hear." (Isaiah 59:1,2). A final truth God wants us to understand with love: "For the wages of sin is death; but the gift of God is eternal life through Jesus Christ our Lord." (Romans 6:23).

How does God feel about sin? He hates it! "And God saw that the wickedness of man was great in the earth and that every imagination of the thoughts of his heart was only evil continually. And it repented the LORD that he had made man on the earth, and it grieved him at his heart." (Genesis 6:5,6). God also said this: "And the LORD said unto Moses, I have seen this people, and, behold, it is a stiffnected (rebellious) people. Now therefore let me alone, that my wrath (anger) may wax hot against them, and that I may consume them; (start all over again) and I will make of thee a great nation." (Exodus 32:9,10). "Say unto them, As I live, saith the Lord God, I have no pleasure in the death of the wicked; but that the wicked turn from his way and live: turn ye from your evil ways; for why will you die, O house of Israel? (Ezekiel 33:11). God loves the sinner and wants to Save the sinner! As mentioned before, God did not make us Robots - He gave us Freedom of choice, He wants us to Love Him, like He Loves us - but, Hates the sin! No Robots in Eternity either, we must be Safe to Save, otherwise, Eternity would be no different than this world. Read God's Promise to us: (Nahum 1:9; Isaiah 11:9).

Satan wants us to Procrastinate (Delay making a decision), None of us are guaranteed another day. We could have a heart attack and die <u>Today.</u> We could be killed in a car accident <u>Today.</u> We could be a victim of a crime <u>Today.</u> We could fall asleep and not wake up <u>Today.</u> Our only Safety is to be right with God <u>Today!</u> In preparing for Eternity, (we, I) need to be aware that our worst enemy is not Satan; **it is unconverted self**, Sin at it's root is self-love--putting self above the will of our Creator. Proverbs 14:12 says, "There is a way which seemeth right unto a man, but the end thereof are the ways of death." Our own ways have fallen so short of finding true happiness and solutions to life's problems. Our Creator knows what is best for us, He made us; His wisdom far exceeds our own. "It is better to trust in the LORD than to put confidence in man." (Psalm 118:8). If you are already a Christian, Do not just go to Church, sing hymns and hear a sermon: read God's Word -The King James Bible, trust and believe Him, and dethrone your worst enemy. "If any man will come after me, let him deny himself and take up his cross, and follow me." (Matthew 16:24). To follow Jesus, is to Read The Bible and ask God for wisdom through the Holy Spirit so we can apply the things we learn to our life. A good Preacher would tell you to read God's Word and obey it! A [really good] Preacher would tell the Brethren what Mary said : "Whatever he (Jesus) saith unto you, do it." (John 2:5).

Remember: B. I. B. L. E. *** Basic - Instructions - Before - Leaving- Earth! ***

Dear [Reader] please go to Amazon Book Store (on-line) Look at the Reviews on my other book - Preparation for Eternity with God by Rick Streight, hope you might want to read that one also! That one concentrates mainly on God's [First Book] The Bible. May God Bless You, sincerely, Rick Martin Streight.

Rick M. Streight

703 Shirley Drive

Aberdeen, Maryland 21001

Phone # 410 - 272 - 0728

COMMENTS OR QUESTIONS WELCOMED !

1. Preparation For Eternity with God by Rick M. Streight

Description: Our time is short on planet earth. Jesus will soon be returning to take His children home...but are we ready? There are preparations we can make. The book you are holding is a story about fighting the good fight of faith and conquering it with Christ's help. God's Word says, "My people are destroyed for lack of knowledge." (Hosea 4:6) The Bible also says, "The truth shall make you free...ye shall be free indeed." (John 8:32,36). Author Rick Streight also speaks about the dangers that surround us, the temptations we often struggle with, and how to overcome sin through Christ.

Available @ Amazon Book Store (on-line)
Available @ Barns and Noble Book Store (on-line)
Available also by Publisher WestBow Press Phone # 1- 866 -928 -1240 .

2. In Defense of the King James Bible by Rick M. Streight

Description: Walk into any bookstore, and you will find a wide variety of Bible translations from which to choose. In Defense of the King James Bible presents a clear scriptural line of reasoning for the unadulterated Word of God, which God said He would preserve. " The words of the LORD are pure words...Thou shalt keep them, O LORD, thou shalt preserve them from this generation for ever." (Psalm 12:6,7). Journey with the author as he examines the Bible to gain a deeper understanding of God's Word and the importance of maintaining the integrity of Jesus Christ who is the Word of God. (John 1:1-3,14 ; Revelation 19: 11-13).

Available @ Amazon Book Store (on -line)
Available @ Barns and Noble Book Store (on -line)
Available also by Publisher - TEACH SERVICES INC. Phone # 1-800 -367 - 1844

Printed in the United States
By Bookmasters